PERFORMANCE EDITIONS

RACHMANINOFF

COMPLETE PRELUDES
Opus 3, Opus 23 and Opus 32

Edited by Alexandre Dossin

The following Schirmer Performance Editions volumes include editor Alexandre Dossin's recordings of the Preludes:

00296858 Rachmaninoff: Preludes, Op. 3 and 23
00296930 Rachmaninoff: Preludes, Op. 32

Alexandre Dossin's recordings of the Rachmaninoff Preludes are also available on iTunes.

T0079529

On the cover:
Between the Waves (1898)
by Ivan Aivazovsky
(1817–1900)

ISBN: 978-1-4803-1262-3

G. SCHIRMER, Inc.

DISTRIBUTED BY

HAL•LEONARD®
CORPORATION
7777 W. BLUEMOUND RD. P.O. BOX 13819 MILWAUKEE, WI 53213

Copyright © 2015 by G. Schirmer, Inc. (ASCAP) New York, NY
International Copyright Secured. All Rights Reserved.

Warning: Unauthorized reproduction of this publication is
prohibited by Federal law and subject to criminal prosecution.

www.musicsalesclassical.com
www.halleonard.com

CONTENTS

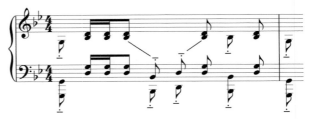

HISTORICAL NOTES

Sergei Rachmaninoff (1873–1943)

Sergei Rachmaninoff was born on one of his grandparents' estates in Oneg, a region of Novgorod in the northwestern part of Russia. [1] Sergei's parents were wealthy landowners and provided him with a comfortable childhood for the first ten years of his life. Financial problems arose due to his father's poor handling of the family affairs which generated a crisis that ended not only in the parents' divorce, but also in a radical change in life style with Sergei and his mother moving to a small flat in Saint Petersburg.

Sergei displayed natural talent for the piano at an early age and his mother arranged for a graduate student at the Saint Petersburg Conservatory to teach him in their home. Rachmaninoff did not do well at the conservatory and, upon the suggestion of his cousin Alexander Siloti, moved to Moscow in 1886, joining the piano studio of Nikolai Zverev. Siloti was already a renowned pianist, having just returned from several years in Weimar, where he studied under Franz Liszt.

Photo credit: George Grantham Bain collection @ wikipedia.com

Nikolai Zverev was a famous pedagogue in Moscow, teaching privately and at the junior division of the Moscow Conservatory. He also kept up to three talented piano students as boarders tuition free. Rachmaninoff joined Matvei Pressman and Leonid Maximov in this capacity. In this new environment, Rachmaninoff spent hours practicing piano and studied other musical subjects.

In 1888, at age 16, Sergei was admitted in the conservatory's senior department as a student of Siloti. Three years later, disagreements between Vladimir Safonov, the powerful new director of the Conservatory, and Alexander Siloti resulted in Siloti's resignation from his post at the Moscow Conservatory. Not interested in changing piano teachers for his last year of study, Rachmaninoff was allowed to finish his studies one year earlier than normal.

Many successful compositions appeared during the early 1890s, including the Prelude in C-sharp minor. In 1897, however, damning reviews of his first symphony drove Rachmaninoff to the edge of depression. For a few years he could not find inspiration to compose and started a conducting career. After consultations with Dr. Nikolai Dahl in psychotherapy sessions that may have involved hypnotic suggestion, Sergei returned to composition with full force and immediately composed several works that became worldwide successes. The list includes the famous Piano Concerto in C minor, one of the most-often performed and recorded concertos in the piano repertoire.

In 1902, Rachmaninoff married his cousin Natalya Satina, and in 1903 their first daughter, Irina, was born. The family was complete in 1907 with the birth of their youngest daughter Tatiana.

The events that culminated in the 1917 revolution in Russia forced Rachmaninoff to emigrate with his young family. Needing to find ways to support his family outside his homeland, Rachmaninoff turned to piano performance as his main source of income. From that period until his death in 1943 he was a constant presence as a celebrated soloist with the best orchestras and in the most important concert venues in Europe and the United States.

Most of his piano works were composed before he left Russia. His only concerto composed after 1917 (No. 4 in G minor, Op. 40) was never received with the same enthusiasm as the previous two concertos (C minor and D minor), and the other two major piano works (*Variations on a Theme by Corelli*, Op. 42 and *Rhapsody on a Theme of Paganini*, Op. 43) are variations on foreign themes. It is almost as if Russia and piano music were so interconnected in his nature that away from his homeland Rachmaninoff could not find the inspiration to compose piano masterworks on his own themes. He never returned to his beloved Russia.

PERFORMANCE NOTES

Rachmaninoff's Piano Music

Fingering

Fingerings are largely editorial and have in mind a medium-sized hand. Some adjustments may be needed for smaller hands. As a rule, fingerings were carefully chosen to convey the phrasing and articulation, not simply for comfort. Two numbers connected by a hyphen represent a slide between black and white keys; two numbers connected by a slur represent finger substitution. In some cases, an optional fingering is shown under or above in parenthesis. When available, Rachmaninoff's own fingerings are shown in italics. Alternate division of notes between hands is indicated by finger brackets.

Pedaling

It is extremely difficult to notate pedaling in an effective way, especially when dealing with such complex pianistic textures as Rachmaninoff's. Good pedaling depends on many variables (quality of the instrument, performer's touch, how far the pedal is pressed, specific acoustics, etc.), that any effort becomes almost pointless, since the performer will need to make the final decisions using his or her musical abilities and sensibilities. Therefore, pedal indications are omitted with the exception of Rachmaninoff's own pedal marking in a few places. It is assumed that performers working on these pieces will have the necessary skills for a successful choice of pedaling. Use the pedal in such a way so the textures are always clear and not compromised by excessive blurring.

Metronome Markings

Metronome markings are original. Rachmaninoff typically did not provide metronome markings for his works; however, the Preludes, Op. 23 are among the few works he did make specific suggestions. His markings are meant only as basic indications of tempo; the music requires a refined flexibility and an organic rubato. In two of the preludes, the metronome indications are very fast and would require utmost virtuosity to project the musical ideas with the necessary clarity at the

suggested tempo (see notes for the A-flat Major and E-flat minor preludes). A review of several recordings shows that in those two particular cases performers do not adhere to Rachmaninoff's original markings. Unfortunately Rachmaninoff did not record those preludes.

Dynamics and Articulation

Dynamics and articulations are Rachmaninoff's. Considered a very thorough proof-reader, Rachmaninoff was very consistent in his writing. There were virtually no inconsistencies in the articulation and phrase markings in the first editions, editions based on autographs, and modern editions. See the notes below on the individual pieces for a discussion on the minor discrepancies between editions.

Rachmaninoff's Preludes

The collection of 24 piano preludes, one in every major and minor key, was not composed at once. The earliest work from this group is the one that has became almost synonymous with Rachmaninoff's name: the celebrated Prelude in C-sharp minor, Op. 3, No. 2, dedicated to his composition teacher, Anton Arensky. Later came ten preludes published as opus 23, composed from 1901–1903. This set is dedicated to his cousin, celebrated pianist Alexander Siloti. Siloti was instrumental not only in Rachmaninoff's piano instruction (first by placing him under Zverev and then as teacher at the Moscow Conservatory) but also in his private life, providing generous financial support to the struggling young composer. Siloti was the first pianist to perform the complete set of the opus 23 preludes in 1904.[2]

In 1910, fresh after his successful tour and premiere of his third piano concerto in the United States, Rachmaninoff completed the final thirteen preludes, published as opus 32. It is assumed that Rachmaninoff came up with the idea of composing a cycle of 24 preludes in all keys mirroring Chopin's set of Preludes, Op. 28, the classic example of this genre, and Scriabin's opus

11 which were very well-received by critics and audiences. It was only natural for Rachmaninoff to contribute to this tradition. The thirteen preludes of opus 32 covered all remaining keys left out of the previous, and returned to the same tonic (D-flat/C-sharp) of the first prelude, ending the set with a broad, cyclical arch.

Notes on the Individual Pieces

Prelude in C-sharp minor, Op. 3, No. 2

One of the pieces included in *Morceaux de fantaisie*, this prelude is certainly the most famous solo piano work written by Rachmaninoff, and a great example of how simplicity generates great works of art. This short piece, only 61 measures long, has many elements of Rachmaninoff's signature style: big chordal textures and huge dynamic contrasts coupled with virtuosic sections and a big culmination. The prelude has become as widely recognized by the piano-loving audiences as Mozart's Turkish March and Beethoven's Für Elise and has made Rachmaninoff a household name.

The musical material of this prelude is very succinct with short motives and a recurrent rhythmic figure. What makes it stand out is Rachmaninoff's brilliant textural creativity. Nicknamed by publishers "The Bells of Moscow," this piece has a resonant bass throughout, and displays a very appealing start, with the descending motive (A–G-sharp–C-sharp) played *fortissimo*. This motive returns repeatedly in the A sections and is the "signature" of the celebrated work. Rachmaninoff himself became tired of it; he was constantly asked to perform it as an encore whenever he concertized.

This is the only prelude for which we have three Rachmaninoff recordings available. The recordings are very helpful when analyzing some discrepancies in the available editions. An important example is found in measures 5 and 48. Many editions include natural signs before the D's in the left hand. This issue has been thoroughly investigated by Hui-Ying Liu-Tawaststjerna. After examining numerous printed editions, she concluded that in 36 editions

> "(…) either a sharp or a natural has been added to the D's. No explanation has been found for why Gutheil's first print (Print A) contains the natural signs. Since Rachmaninoff himself played D-sharps in his recordings—the way it is indicated in his autograph—the D-naturals must be

considered engraver's mistakes. To correct this error, Gutheil presumably replaced all the naturals with sharps in the subsequent prints." [3]

Another example is found in measures 6 and 49. In the original manuscript, there are G-sharp Major chords in the beginning of the measures. However, all editions omit the sharp signs. According to Dr. Tawaststjerna,

> "it is assumed here therefore that Rachmaninoff gave his consent, before the first edition was printed, to replace all the G-sharp Major chords with G-sharp minor ones, an assumption that seems to be confirmed by Rachmaninoff's recorded performances of this Prelude." [4]

The performer of this prelude will be confronted with several challenges: textural control in the first section, virtuosic passages in the middle section, and heavy chords played by both hands, using the entire keyboard range in the recapitulation of the main section.

Preludes, Opus 23

Prelude in F-sharp minor, Op. 23, No. 1

The set of ten preludes begins with an ominous, dark piece. The main challenge to the performer is the polyphonic texture, requiring advanced control of touch, dynamics, and articulation. The musical language—highly chromatic and with scant melodic material—will return in Rachmaninoff's work more than once. One clear example is from variation XVII of *Rhapsody on a Theme of Paganini* for piano and orchestra, composed in 1934. Pedal should be used with great care, keeping the three main textural layers well defined. Use arm weight to project the long melodic notes and a distinction between finger and wrist weight in the left-hand accompaniment figure. The left-hand chords in measures 39–41 require a very large hand with a span of an octave between fingers 5 and 2. Instead of rolling the chords, I suggest omitting the second F-sharp from the bottom. There are still three F-sharps in the chord, so the difference in sound will be minimal with no loss for the final, tonic quality of the chords.

Prelude in B-flat Major, Op. 23, No. 2

The contrast could not be bigger. The prelude begins with "all stops pulled" and a rich sound, exploring a wide range of the keyboard. It is a tour de force for the left hand with textures that are typical in Rachmaninoff's music: a mix of scales and arpeggios encompassing several octaves in a few beats. The "bell" sound is very obvious in this piece, and one of the main challenges that confront the player is how to maintain a strong sound (*ff, sempre marcato*) without forcing it. The middle section begins in measure 8 with a two-measure weakening of the sound. The entrance of a powerful tenor line at the end of measure 19 brings some variety to the texture. The bells in the right hand give way to a melody which is full of Russian melancholy. Rachmaninoff's use of the keyboard proves once more his mastery of the instrument. Three distinct layers permeate this section, challenging the pianist to keep perfect control of touch throughout. After the "soft culmination" in measure 27, the performer is confronted with a rhythmically complex section, requiring independence of hands. One should be able to listen to each hand as if coming from different stereophonic speakers instead of trying to synchronize one to the other. After several measures using imitation technique, the listener is prepared for the triumphant return of the main section.

The return of the A section is an exact repeat of the first 17 measures and the coda begins in measure 54. It has a scintillating, shimmering quality, with high-register 32nd notes in the right hand that brings the piece to a brilliant end in a bravura display of octaves.

Prelude in D minor, Op. 23, No. 3

This prelude displays a different style from the typical Rachmaninoff texture, full of cascades of notes. Instead, we are transported to an almost baroque feeling with a dance-like, chordal texture marked *Tempo di minuetto* by Rachmaninoff. This prelude is more understated when compared to the previous prelude; a *fortissimo* is briefly reached in m. 35, but does not last for very long. The challenge of the prelude is, in a way, the opposite of the previous prelude. The pianist here is challenged to keep a moderate sound for a long time while maintaining the distinction between the layers. The texture is at times polyphonic (mm. 18–20 and mm. 22–28), and some intervals require a large span for the left hand (m. 31). The energetic motive that appears at the beginning (the 32nd-note triplets in the left hand of measures 2 and 4) is a very important element in the musical discourse of this small but powerful piece. The motive contrasts with the static eighth-note chords of the first measure on three levels:

dynamic, rhythmic and melodic. This motive returns several times and can also be recognized in an augmented form in measures 18 and 22 in the left hand. Motivic unity is very clear in this prelude. Notice how the culminating measures (mm. 35–45) repeat over and over the melodic material from the first theme in diminution, while immediately contrasting it with the motive in 32nd-note triplets. The coda, beginning in measure 55, requires the use of the sostenuto pedal to sustain the tonic note for several measures while maintaining clarity in the remaining layers.

Prelude in D Major, Op. 23, No. 4

Long melodic material, well-delineated accompaniment surrounding the melody, and rich harmonies are the winning ingredients of this expressive masterpiece. Even though it is possible to use the original hand distribution, we suggest fingering and strategic placement of hand positions based on a very smooth, *cantabile* right hand. Of course this solution creates other challenges, such as the need to voice evenly the accompaniment material between hands. The repeat of the main theme beginning in measure 19 separates the texture in three clear layers: the melodic in the middle, surrounded by a counter melody in the top and the arpeggiated accompaniment in the left hand. In the middle section, long melodic lines create waves that reach the softest point (m. 43) before building to the climax in measure 51 which leads to the return of the A section in yet one more textural variation. The theme is now presented in chords, with a syncopated counter melody on the weak part of the beat a sixth above the theme. Rachmaninoff believed in the importance of finding a culminating point in each piece (*totchka* in Russian) for a successful performance. In this prelude, one could argue that there are two such points, one soft (*pp*, m. 43), and one loud (m. 51). For a successful performance, both places should be brought out in a special way. A tasteful use of *rubato* will be necessary throughout.

Prelude in G minor, Op. 23, No. 5

After the Prelude in C-sharp minor, Op. 3, No. 2, the G-minor prelude is the most famous. The reasons are clear: exciting rhythm, rich textures, virtuosic chordal sections, brilliant octaves, and a middle section that could be written only by Rachmaninoff. The performer of this prelude will be confronted with numerous pianistic challenges:

repeated chords in various dynamic levels, complex articulation (*staccato* in one hand with *legato* in the other in places like measures 7 and 8), and several other difficulties. The middle section, rich in melodic and harmonic content, requires a good control of *legato* in the large chords of the right hand, and fluent left-hand arpeggios. As usual in Rachmaninoff's piano music, the amount of notes to be played is by itself a challenge; however, one should avoid a performance that only displays the many notes, and should instead follow the original slurs that show clearly how many notes should be played under one gesture.

This is one of the preludes for which we have an original Rachmaninoff recording. Interestingly enough, he adds two extra notes at the end of the prelude. Those notes are not found in the autograph nor in the editions printed during his lifetime. This is the first prelude of this set Rachmaninoff wrote, composed in 1901.

Prelude in E-flat Major, Op. 23, No. 6

This Prelude is a great example of Rachmaninoff's masterly writing for the left hand. According to Julian Haylock, this prelude was composed on the day his first daughter, Irina, was born.[5] It is a beautiful, waving melody that at the same time complements wonderfully the right-hand melodic/harmonic texture. In a fascinating way, this prelude inverts the normal texture with a chordal right hand accompanied by a melodic left hand. Similarly to No. 4, this short masterpiece has two clear culminating points: a loud one (*f*, m. 19) and a soft one (*pp*, m. 28). Both should be carefully prepared, for without a successful execution of these passages, the piece looses its effect. The rather detailed and specific fingering offered is geared towards a fluent and expressive rendition of the left-hand melody.

Prelude in C minor, Op. 23, No. 7

Bells return with full force in this virtuosic prelude. Composed in the same key as the famous Piano Concerto No. 2, the prelude displays non-stop motion, *moto perpetuo*, in sixteenth notes. The texture is cleverly built, resulting in a clear "three-hands effect." The fast tempo required by Rachmaninoff (MM = 80 for the half-note) will only work with a clear definition between sixteenth notes, quarter notes, and also half notes marked in the score. These notes delineate hidden motives that are also present in the sixteenth notes.

The pianist needs to access the reverberation of the instrument when choosing the appropriate touch. Pedal should be generously used, but a thick sound will create a blurry texture.

Prelude in A-flat Major, Op. 23, No. 8

This is another prelude requiring extreme dexterity in the right hand. Rachmaninoff's metronome marking (MM = 108 for the half note), with a texture of non-stop sixteenth notes throughout, is almost impossible to reach. At MM = 216 for each quarter note, this would require an astounding rate of about 12 notes per second! Most recordings do not reach that speed, going to a maximum of MM = 180 for the quarter note (still a remarkable feat). In order to achieve the fast tempo required, even if under Rachmaninoff's original tempo, one needs to differentiate clearly between the quarter notes (marked with stems down) and the accompanying sixteenth notes. They should be played in the same gesture as the quarter notes; a supple wrist will do the trick. Special textural control will be necessary in the section from measure 32 until measure 42. The dynamic markings (mostly *pp*) coupled with the proximity between the layers require a very careful and light touch. The long notes in the left hand cannot be held with the finger alone since the right hand also uses the same keys. The only solution is a very refined use of the pedal.

Prelude in E-flat minor, Op. 23, No. 9

Definitely the hardest in this set, this reminds one of Liszt's famous "Feux-Folets" from the *Transcendental Études*, and to a less extent, Schumann's Toccata, Op. 7. Unlike Liszt, though, Rachmaninoff uses fast double notes throughout the piece in a real *perpetuum mobile* tour de force. Here again, the metronome marking is almost impossible to achieve. Of all recordings researched, most pianists stay under the required MM = 152 for the quarter note. Of course, all recordings use some *rubato*, but the average tempo in those recordings varies from MM = 120–140. Unfortunately, Rachmaninoff did not record this prelude. It is interesting to note that Liszt's metronome marking is MM = 120–126 for the eighth-note ("Feux-Folets" is written in 2/4, with thirty-second notes instead of sixteenth notes). Even at that speed, "Feux-Folets" is considered one of the hardest works in the piano repertoire. The overall dynamic of Rachmaninoff's Prelude in E-flat minor is *p–pp*, with a few outbursts of *f* and *mf*. A light legato touch with the fingers very close to the key (not really allowing the keys to go all the way up), will help with the speed and texture. Be prepared for hours and hours of practice to be culminated in only 2 minutes of performance.

Prelude in G-flat Major, Op. 23, No. 10

The opus 23 group of Preludes ends softly with this inspired, short piece. After the difficult texture found in the Prelude in E-flat minor, this one may seem at first glance technically easy. In fact, the thick texture of the last section (beginning in m. 47) is the only moment when the performer is asked to display some technical expertise. However, musical challenges abound: long melodic notes in the left hand are accompanied by melodic-like chords in the right hand. Not surprisingly, this prelude exists in a version for cello and piano. Starting in measure 9, the texture is expanded to include a conversation between left and right hands, accompanied by chords in the middle register. It is very important to give each layer its own color, presenting all layers with great clarity. Rachmaninoff's recording of this prelude is very expressive and free, with a decisive *accelerando* and *crescendo* in the middle section (mm. 19–30), and a refined control of layers. He adds a B-flat in the right hand (m. 55), not found in any of the available editions. Rachmaninoff also ends the prelude quietly, contrary to most editions, which have a f above the last two chords. Only the 2006 Russian Music Publishing/Bärenreiter edition indicates p for these chords.

Preludes, Opus 32

In a letter to Morozov written on July 31, 1910 mentioning his summer work, Rachmaninoff comments: ". . . worst of all goes the business of the little piano pieces . . ." [6] These preludes were written in the keys necessary to complete a cycle of twenty four preludes which included the ten preludes from opus 23 and the Prelude in C-sharp minor, Op. 3, No. 2. During the same period, Rachmaninoff composed a sacred choral work, the *Liturgy of St John Chrysostom*, Op. 31 and a group of etudes, published in 1911 as *Etudes-Tableaux*, Op. 33.

The years between the composition of preludes from opus 23 and opus 32 were years of travel for Rachmaninoff. After spending some time in Italy, Germany and a grueling tour in the United States, Rachmaninoff and his family settled on the Ivanovka estate.

Considering the pianistic style of both sets of preludes, one could make a broad comparison, relating opus 23 to the second piano concerto and opus 32 to the third piano concerto. The texture in the preludes opus 32 tends to be more complex, polyphonic, and display motivic phrasing, a characteristic already shown in the first set, but taken here to new proportions.

It is interesting to observe a couple of textural elements that permeate this set, making it more unified than opus 23. One of the most important is the rhythmic figure

which is found in almost every measure of the Preludes in B-flat minor and B Major. The motive also has an important role in the Prelude in B minor (mm. 1–19 and the return of the same theme after the cadenza in m. 49). This rhythmic figure also appears briefly in the Prelude in D-flat Major (mm. 11–17), and in a less obvious way, augmented in the initial octaves of the Prelude in E minor. Another interesting feature is Rachmaninoff's use of repeated, large chords, combined with strong bass notes to create culminating moments. Clear examples of these can be found in the Prelude in B minor (mm. 18–36) and the Prelude in D-flat Major (mm. 40–41).

Prelude in C Major, Op. 32, No. 1

Only 41 measures long and under 2 minutes of performance time, this is one of the shortest preludes in this set. It brings to mind Chopin's short Prelude in C Major, Op. 28, No. 1 as well as Liszt's first transcendental etude. A hint of the descending main motive (A–G-sharp–C-sharp) from Rachmaninoff's famous Prelude in C-sharp minor, Op. 3, No. 2 is present here, transposed to C minor:

Apart from the relationship to the Prelude in C-sharp minor, Op. 3, No. 2, there is also a relationship to the last prelude in D-flat Major. It gives a nice sense of proportion and even a cyclical feeling to the set of 24 preludes. As usual, in Rachmaninoff's piano music, the technical difficulties are pianistic, and it takes just an initial play-through to feel that sense of comfort. In contrast to opus 23, where original fingerings were kept to a minimum, in opus 32 Rachmaninoff wrote very detailed fingering. Quite often, however, the original fingering becomes very difficult or impossible for someone with small hands. Rachmaninoff's hands were not only very large, but he also had an incredible span between his fingers. Rachmaninoff's suggested fingering for the right hand in measure 22 is a good example: a diminished seventh played with fingers 3 and 5. Pay attention to the composer's articulation indications in the beginning (mm. 1–4 and similar), using the wrist to perform the short, repeated thirds.

Prelude in B-flat minor, Op. 32, No. 2

After spending several months working in the composition of a sacred work (*Liturgy of St John Chrysostom*, Op. 31), it is only natural that some religious character transpires in other pieces. This is the case with the Prelude in B-flat minor. The ostinato rhythm that permeates this reflective prelude (present in each measure with the exception of mm. 32–35) will be used again in the Preludes in B minor and D-flat Major. The section beginning in m. 17 starts a wave-like *crescendo* (from *pp–mf*, then from *p–ff*) and *accelerando*, culminating in a dramatic, two-measure *ff* (mm. 25–26). Throughout the prelude, lean a little on the first note of the dotted-rhythm motive, playing all three notes under one gesture. In the *allegro* section, use wrist rotation and pivoting fingers.

Prelude in E Major, Op. 32, No. 3

The religious character continues with this joyous prelude, bringing out one of Rachmaninoff's musical signatures: bells, bells and more bells! The performer of this prelude is challenged to display great dynamic contrasts, from *ff* to *pp*. A wise use of pedal will help create the necessary ringing sound. Flexible wrists will keep the loud chords moving and horizontal. Don't fall for a typical mistake in this prelude: playing it too loud and too vertical. Bells ring and move. Make your chords do the same. Rachmaninoff's fingering for the left hand in measure 6 and similar places once again reflects the large span of his hand. Playing the last beat of this measure with the implied 1-2-4-5 fingering (resulting in a sixth between G-sharp and B to be reached by fingers 2 and 4), especially at a fast speed, is very uncomfortable for a normally-sized hand. The suggested fingering (1-2-5-4) allows for a better rotation and more hand stability.

Prelude in E minor, Op. 32, No. 4

One of the longest (158 measures, including the alternate *ossia* ending) and certainly the most difficult in this set, this prelude shows Rachmaninoff in his best symphonic style. The texture is layered, with distinctive, orchestral sonorities. Use your imagination and create your own orchestration (after listening to Rachmaninoff's orchestral music first) for this magnificent and powerful piece. The mood varies from majestic (trumpet beginning) to *scherzando* (section beginning in m. 27), to lyrical (*Lento* section, beginning in m. 53, which includes the measures with the thickest texture, mm. 62–70), culminating in a triumphant, *presto possible* section, with full chords played *fortissimo*. Only play this one if you feel really at ease with octaves and fast chordal textures. I suggest using the longer version (*ossia*) to end the prelude, where a quote from the oft-quoted *Dies irae* gives an extra religious touch to this powerful piece.

Prelude in G Major, Op. 32, No. 5

A bird song by a stream would be a suitable description of this charming prelude. The irregular rhythm—quintuplets in the left hand accompanying triplets in the right hand—resembles the freedom of nature, where nothing is standard, but everything is proportional. Here the pianist is required to have complete rhythmic control, keeping the pulse steady with a slight *rubato* and allowing both hands to live "parallel lives." In the left hand, use some arm weight for the quarter notes while playing the remaining four notes of the quintuplets gently using only fingers; use a more intense arm weight to project the melody even at the *pp* level. The thirty-second note *leggiero* little turns should be played with the tips of the fingers and a fast but soft attack, creating a bright, while still soft sonority.

Prelude in F minor, Op. 32, No. 6

Another short *tour de force*, and to a certain extent similar to the initial Prelude in C Major. This prelude/etude is based on concise motives and never develops memorable melodic content. The piece requires dexterity and comfortable knowledge of the keyboard topography due to its use of the entire range of the instrument. In order to keep an appropriate balance between the layers, make sure that the sixteenth notes are light so the longer notes, especially the dotted quarter notes, can be expressive. Rachmaninoff was a very careful proof-reader of his scores, and printing mistakes are rare, especially when one considers the textural complexity of his music. One minor exception may be present in this prelude (see also notes for the Prelude in A minor); the section from m. 53 to 57 at the end of this prelude is marked by a powerful descending line in the left hand, a series of minor thirds:

In all editions reviewed, the third eight note in the left hand of measure 55 is A-flat, breaking the sequence. The correct note for the sequence to work would be F. A-flat also removes one of the characteristics of the F-minor triad in that passage, adding the third of the triad, where the other similar moments employ an empty triad without its third. The editor believes this to be an error not noticed by Rachmaninoff and perpetuated in all subsequent editions. Rachmaninoff's performance of this prelude "corrects" the error.

Prelude in F Major, Op. 32, No. 7

This prelude has a generally peaceful mood, but hints of uneasiness abound: intriguing harmonies, off-beat accompaniment chords, syncopations—all these elements help contribute to the ambiguous atmosphere of this interesting piece, which is unfortunately not performed as often as it should. Not technically demanding, it still poses some challenges, mainly related to voicing control, skips and the need for extended reach in certain chords. Once again, Rachmaninoff composed this piece with his hand size in mind. This edition suggests a different hand distribution that helps to bring out the polyphonic texture of this piece for pianists with a medium-sized hand. Rachmaninoff's inspiring recording of this prelude shows him in full control of *rubato*, with a clear definition of layers.

Prelude in A minor, Op. 32, No. 8

Similar to the Prelude in F minor, this piece is short, powerful, and in the style of an etude. It requires dexterity and great cross-hands technique. In this prelude, the editor believes that a minor error has been perpetuated through editions. This concerns m. 35 where right hand has a pattern of minor thirds followed by an octave. Most editions (with the exception of Dover and Masters Music, both reprints of early Russian editions) print a tenth (A-C) as the last right-hand sixteenth note:

The logical continuation would be an octave C-C, keeping the pattern and not adding a large interval in the middle of a very fast passage. There is not a recording of Rachmaninoff available for this prelude, and the passage is so fast that one can not clearly identify which notes, A or C, pianists usually perform. The editor suggests playing an octave. If you decide to keep with the original notation but are not able to reach a tenth at fast tempo, one solution would be to play the A with left hand. Notice that in the last measure, *f* applies only to the second beat; the first beat is still *pp*.

Prelude in A Major, Op. 32, No. 9

This prelude has the typical "Rachmaninoff warmth," with lush sonorities and a rich texture. The undulating octave line in the low register supports the rhythmic *ostinato* in the middle (one could call it the piece's "heartbeat"), both preparing the stage for the beautiful melody, marked **mf**. This melodic line, in its simplicity and depth, is formed by a downward leap of a sixth followed by a scale moving up. The editor suggests performing the *ossia* (mm. 15–17 and 19–20); they add a little difficulty to that section, but the effort is worthwhile. The ascending quadruplets add to the rhythmic drive, and the arrivals (second beats of mm. 17 and 21) become more pronounced and exciting. After a brief return of the main idea in the minor mode (mm. 29–30) and its quick tonal transitions through A-flat Major and F-sharp minor, we arrive at a fast, virtuosic passage (*Più vivo*) that obsessively repeats the falling initial sixths. Use wrist rotation in the right hand to avoid performing mm. 41–49 with fingers only.

Prelude in B minor, Op. 32, No. 10

Together with the Prelude in E minor and the Prelude in D-flat Major, this is one of the longest in the set. It is a well-known fact that Rachmaninoff drew inspiration from a painting by Swiss symbolist painter Arnold Böcklin titled *Die Heimkehr* (*The Return* or *The Homecoming*), reproduced on the front cover of this edition. This is the second time Rachmaninoff used a Böcklin painting as inspiration. He had previously based his symphonic work *Isle of the Dead*, Op. 29 on a Böcklin painting. The static character of this somber prelude brings to mind Liszt's "Il Penseroso," a piano work that also has extra-musical inspiration (based on a sculpture by Michelangelo). Unlike Liszt's work, this prelude is extended and includes a big culminating, chordal section (mm. 22–36), as well as a virtuosic passage (mm. 47–48) before returning to the starting mood. The main challenges in this prelude are textural; a successful performance of this piece will require full control of dynamics and a deep tonal control. From the very beginning, differentiate the dotted-rhythm motif from the accompanying chords. In the culminating section (mm. 22–36), play the melody with your whole upper torso while vibrating the repeated chords, keeping your hands close to the keys. This will create a full sound with a variety of colors, avoiding falling in the typical trap of being too loud for too long. Don't forget Rachmaninoff's "*tochka*": define the culminating point clearly for a successful and satisfying performance.

Prelude in B Major, Op. 32, No. 11

This peaceful and almost religious work is unusual in its textural simplicity, when compared to most other preludes by Rachmaninoff. It is chordal from the beginning to the end, not using any of the typical pianistic richness one expects from Rachmaninoff. It brings to mind the Prelude in D minor, Op. 23, No. 3. Several of the same skills are needed for a successful performance: good rhythmic and voicing control, plus the ability to play "horizontally" in a "vertical" texture. In order to enhance the richness of sound, pay special attention to the lowest and highest notes in each chord, creating a frame for it. Another challenge in this piece is the phrasing, which requires complete independence between the hands; in the right hand, slurs in some instances cover two measures (mm. 3–4, 7–8), while sometimes only one measure (mm. 9, 10, 11, 12), or connect partial measures (mm. 23–24, 24–25). Quite often, the left hand has slurs that don't match those of right hand, creating a very interesting, polyphonic phrasing.

Prelude in G-sharp minor, Op. 32, No. 12

One of the most often performed preludes in opus 32, this work is a masterpiece of conciseness. In only 48 measures and just over 2 minutes of performance time, Rachmaninoff is able to portray the beauty and vastness of his homeland. It could be interpreted as a description of winter: the coldness of the open fifth initial *arpeggio*, its fast motion and *crescendo* feeling like freezing

wind; this contrasts with the warm melody played by left hand symbolizing someone confronting the elements, bringing human warmth to a cold landscape. Rachmaninoff's detailed tempo indications, almost in each measure, should be carefully followed, creating an organic *rubato*. Texturally, this prelude shows Rachmaninoff's wonderful control of the keyboard. The entire piece falls naturally under the fingers: the *ostinato* sixteenth notes are almost always played within one octave, while the left-hand melody is built mainly of small intervals. In measure 18 (fourth beat of the left hand), most editions omit a natural sign before the B. The harmonic motion of the previous two measures suggests that the chords in the fourth beats are followed by 4 sixteenth notes in the same harmony (observe the fourth beats of mm. 16 and 17). In the editor's opinion, a natural sign is needed in m. 18 in order for the harmony to remain consistent. There is not a Rachmaninoff recording of this prelude; however, in most recordings surveyed, pianists perform B natural.

Prelude in D-flat Major, Op. 32, No. 13

The last prelude is one of the longest and certainly one of the hardest. It brings back some thematic and rhythmic ideas from previous preludes; the rhythm in mm. 11–17 reminds one of the Prelude in B-flat minor and the Prelude in B Major, while the repeated *ff* chords of mm. 40–41 are similar to the long culminating section in the Prelude in B minor (see mm. 18–36 of that prelude). The most important and remarkable "flashback" is the return of the famous three-note motive from the Prelude in C-sharp minor, Op. 3, No. 2. The quote starts to appear in m. 31 in the left hand. The intervallic relationship is still not the exact one and the rhythm is still dotted. Beginning in m. 37, however, it is repeated 4 times in the original form. The famous A–G-sharp–C-sharp motive (mm. 37–39) is shown in an augmented form in the bass (mm. 40–42), culminating with the recapitulation of the main theme.

This prelude, with all its textural richness and harmonic warmth, ends the group of 24 preludes in an almost cyclical way. The pianistic texture in the section from mm. 21–26, with its right-hand polyphonic conversation supported by a low and undulating bass line, will be used in later pieces such as the Etude-tableaux in E-flat minor, Op. 39, No. 5. The return of the main theme in m. 42 is very full, with a thick texture. Extended chords abound (see mm. 46–49), and are impossible to perform blocked, as written. This edition suggests a different hand distribution and even omitting certain notes in cases when they are duplicated in the chords. The rhythm in m. 60 should be felt in eight notes, and the extended chords can be performed with the fingering suggested.

Notes:

[1] There has been confusion about Rachmaninoff's real birthplace. He always mentioned Oneg as his birthplace, but some scholars believe he was born at Semyonovo, and moved to Oneg because of his father's unfortunate financial decisions.

[2] Several sources indicate February 10, 1903 as the first complete performance of opus 23. However, according to Apetian (*Rachmaninoff: Letters*, p. 222), only three preludes were performed by the composer on that day: Prelude in F-sharp minor, B-flat Major, and G minor. Siloti's performance of opus 23, according to Antipov, was on November 13, 1904, in Saint Petersburg.

[3] Tawaststjerna, p. 40.

[4] ibid., p. 41.

[5] "A baby daughter, Irina, was born on May 14, in response to which Rachmaninov sat down the very same day and composed his *E flat Major Prelude* (no. 6), a microcosm of wide-eyed innocence and blissful contentment." Haylock, p. 33.

[6] Bertensson and Leyda, p. 168.

Editions Consulted:

Prelude, Op. 3, No. 2

Rachmaninoff, Sergei. *Prelude in C-sharp minor, Op. 3, No. 2*. London: Boosey & Hawkes, 1893.

Rachmaninoff, Sergei. *Prelude in C-sharp minor, Op. 3, No. 2*. Edited by Louis Oesterle. New York: G. Schirmer, Inc., 1898 (renewed, 1925).

Rachmaninoff, Sergei. *Prelude in C-sharp minor, Op. 3, No. 2*. Milan: Casa Ricordi, 1936.

Rachmaninoff, Sergei. *Prelude in C-sharp minor, Op. 3, No. 2*. Mainz, Germany: Schott Music, 1961.

Rachmaninoff, Sergei. *Prelude in C-sharp minor, Op. 3, No. 2: Facsimile*. Moscow: State Publishers, Muzika, 1977.

Rachmaninoff, Sergei. *Prelude in C-sharp minor, Op. 3, No. 2*. Budapest, Hungary: Editio Musica Budapest, 2006.

Prelude, Op. 3, No. 2 as part of *Fantasy Pieces*, Op. 3

Rachmaninoff, Sergei. *Fantasy Pieces, Op. 3*. Edited by Murray Baylor. Van Nuys, California: Alfred Music Publishing, 1986.

Rachmaninoff, Sergei. *Fantasy Pieces, Op. 3*. Boca Raton, Florida: Master Music Publications, 1992.

Prelude, Op. 23, No. 5

Rachmaninoff, Sergei. *Prelude in G minor, Op. 23, No. 5*. Edited by Louis Oesterle. New York: G. Schirmer, Inc., 1904.

Rachmaninoff, Sergei. *Prelude in G minor, Op. 23, No. 5*. London: Boosey & Hawkes, 1904.

Rachmaninoff, Sergei. *Prelude in G minor, Op. 23, No. 5*. Edited by Murray Baylor. Van Nuys, California: Alfred Music Publishing, 1987.

Preludes, Op. 32

Rachmaninoff, Sergei. *Preludes for the Piano, Op. 32*. New York: G. Schirmer, Inc., 1942.

Rachmaninoff, Sergei. *Thirteen Preludes, Opus 32*. Edited by Ruth Laredo. New York: Edition Peters, 1990.

Preludes, Op. 23

Rachmaninoff, Sergei. *Preludes Op. 23*. Moscow: A. Gutheil, 1904.

Rachmaninoff, Sergei. *Preludes Op. 23*. New York: G. Schirmer, Inc., 1904.

Rachmaninoff, Sergei. *Preludes Op. 23*. Moscow: Muzgiz, ca. 1948.

Rachmaninoff, Sergei. *Preludes Op. 23*. Edited by Murray Baylor. Van Nuys, California: Alfred Music Publishing, 1987.

Rachmaninoff, Sergei. *Preludes Op. 23*. Moscow: "Kristina" Publishing House, 1992.

Rachmaninoff, Sergei. *Preludes Op. 23*. Saint Petersburg: "Kompozitor" Publishing House, 1993.

Complete Preludes, Op. 3, No. 2; Op. 23; and Op. 32

Rachmaninoff, Sergei. *Preludes Op. 3 No. 2, Op. 23 and Op. 32*. Van Nuys, California: Alfred Music Publishing, 1988.

Rachmaninoff, Sergei. *Preludes Op. 3 No. 2, Op. 23 and Op. 32*. Edited by Robert Threlfall. London: Boosey & Hawkes, 1992.

Rachmaninoff, Sergei. *Preludes Op. 3 No. 2, Op. 23 and Op. 32*. New York: G. Schirmer, Inc., 1994.

Rachmaninoff, Sergei. *Preludes Op. 3 No. 2, Op. 23 and Op. 32*. Moscow: Russian Music Publishing/ Bärenreiter, 2006.

Bibliography:

Apetian, Zarui, editor. *S.V. Rachmaninoff: Pis'ma*. Moscow: State Musical Publisher, 1955.

Bertensson, Sergei, and Jay Leyda. *Sergei Rachmaninoff: A Lifetime in Music*. New York: New York University Press, 1956.

Haylock, Julian. *Sergei Rachmaninov: An Essential Guide to His Life and Works*. London: Pavilion Books 1997.

Lui-Tawaststjerna, Hui-Ying. *Rachmaninoff's Prelude in C-sharp minor, Op. 3, No 2: The Composer's Notation and His Three Interpretations*. Helsinki: Sibelius Academy, 2004.

Norris, Geoffrey. *Rakhmaninov*. London: J. M. Dent & Sons Ltd, 1976.

Scott, Michael. *Rachmaninoff*. Stroud, Gloucestershire: The History Press Ltd., 2008.

Seroff, Victor I. *Rachmaninoff* . New York: Books for Libraries Press, 1950.

à Monsieur A. Arensky

Prelude in C-sharp Minor

from *Morceaux de fantaisie*

Sergei Rachmaninoff
Op. 3, No. 2

*Optional fingering mm. 2–11:   **See introductory notes.   ***See introductory notes.

Copyright © 2012 by G. Schirmer, Inc. (ASCAP) New York, NY
International Copyright Secured. All Rights Reserved.

* in manuscript.

Tempo I

*$\begin{array}{c}\text{[musical notation]}\end{array}$ and $\begin{array}{c}\text{[musical notation]}\end{array}$ in manuscript. All other editions add the fourth note.

**See introductory notes.

*See note for mm. 2–11.
**See note for mm. 47–48.

à Monsieur A. Siloti

Preludes, Op. 23
I

Sergei Rachmaninoff
Op. 23, No. 1

Copyright © 2012 by G. Schirmer, Inc. (ASCAP) New York, NY
International Copyright Secured. All Rights Reserved.

*See introductory notes.

II

Sergei Rachmaninoff
Op. 23, No. 2

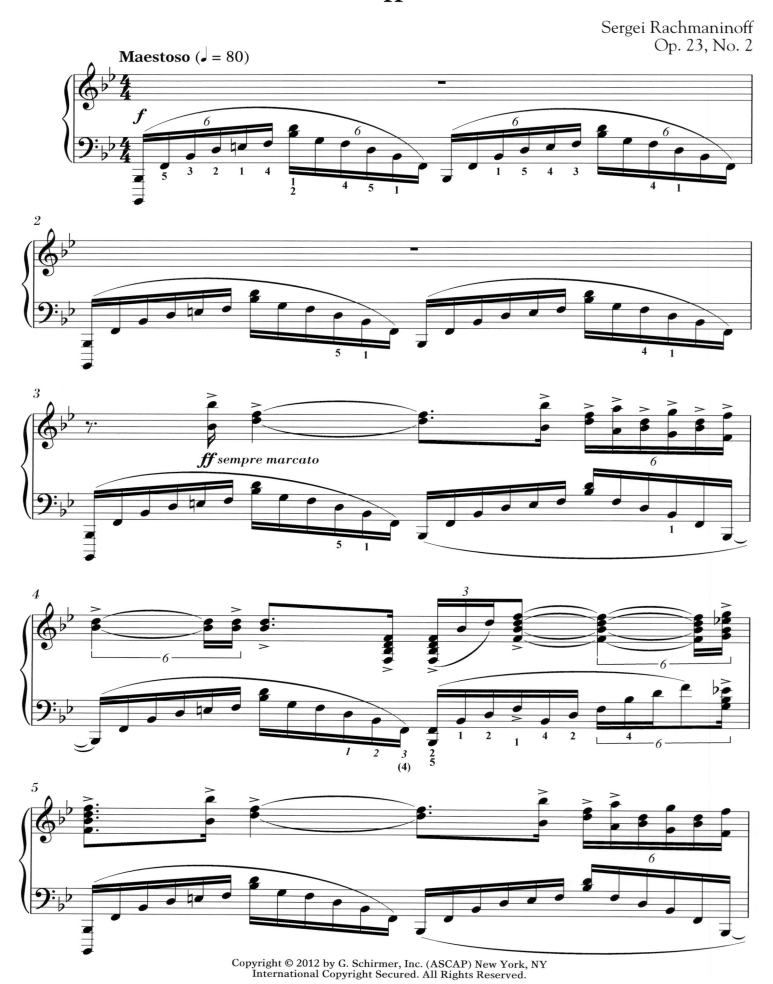

Copyright © 2012 by G. Schirmer, Inc. (ASCAP) New York, NY
International Copyright Secured. All Rights Reserved.

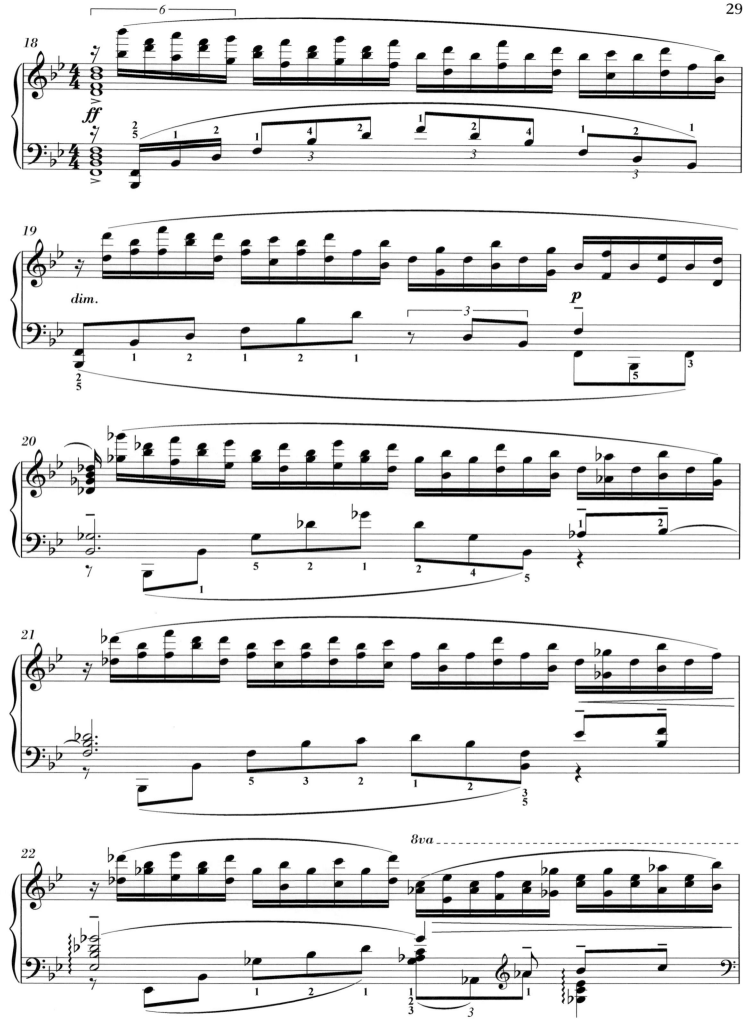

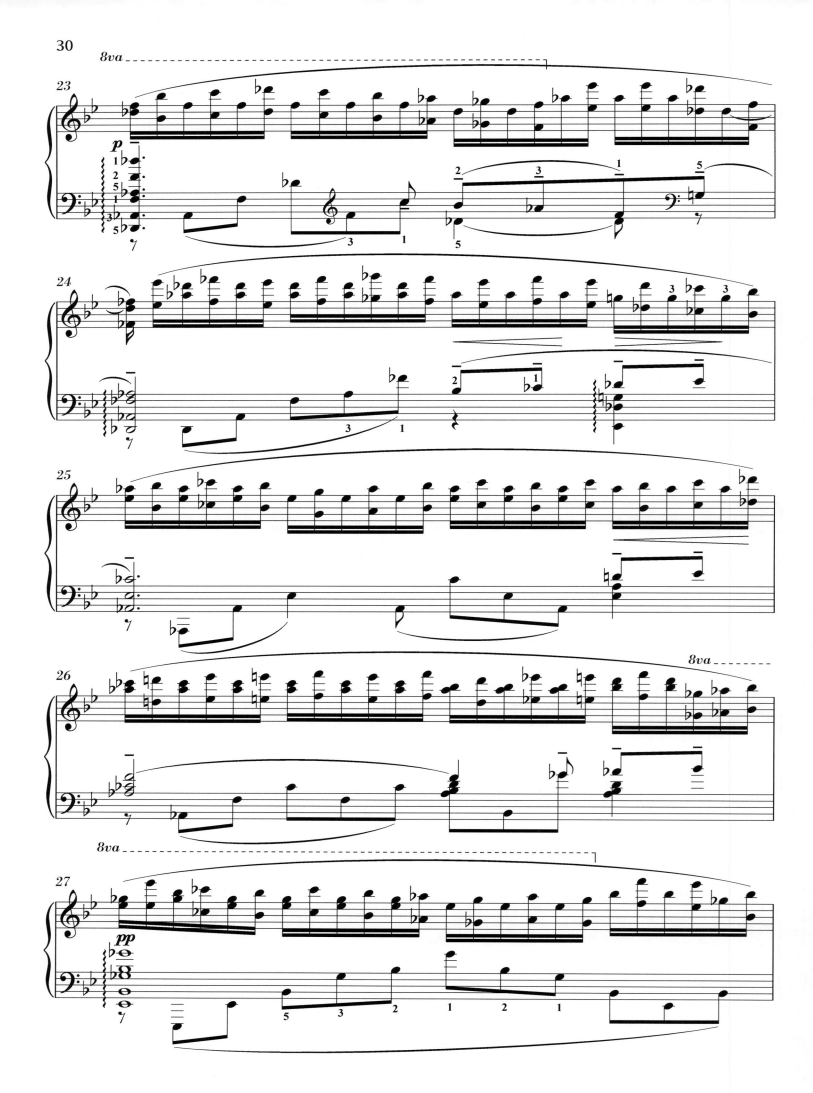

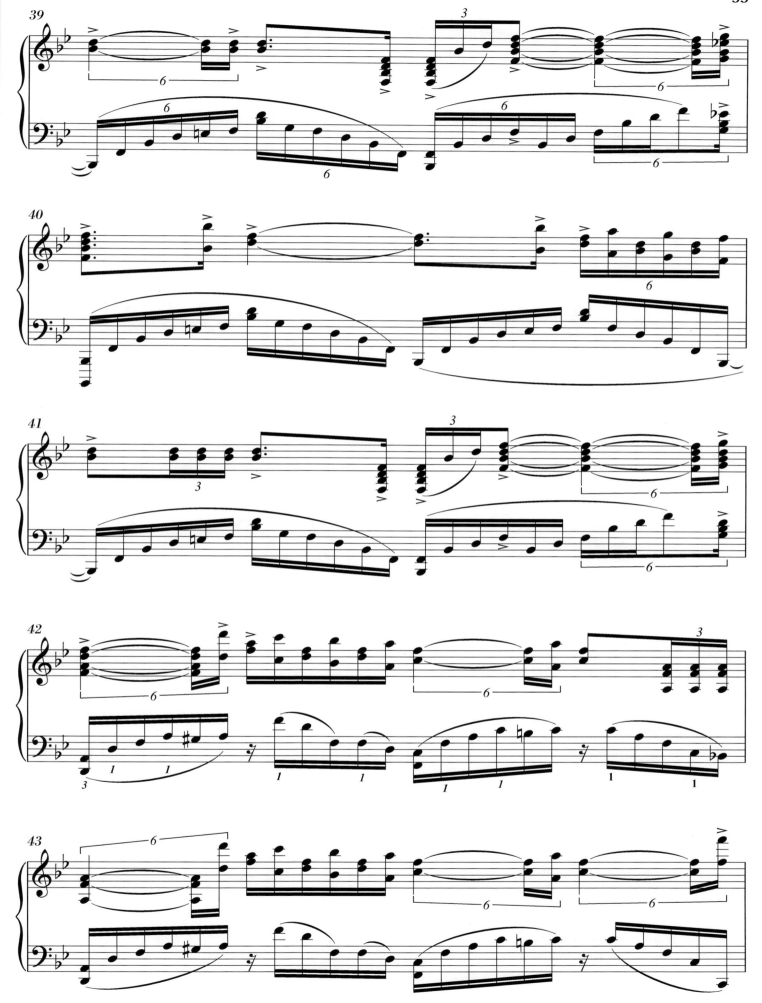

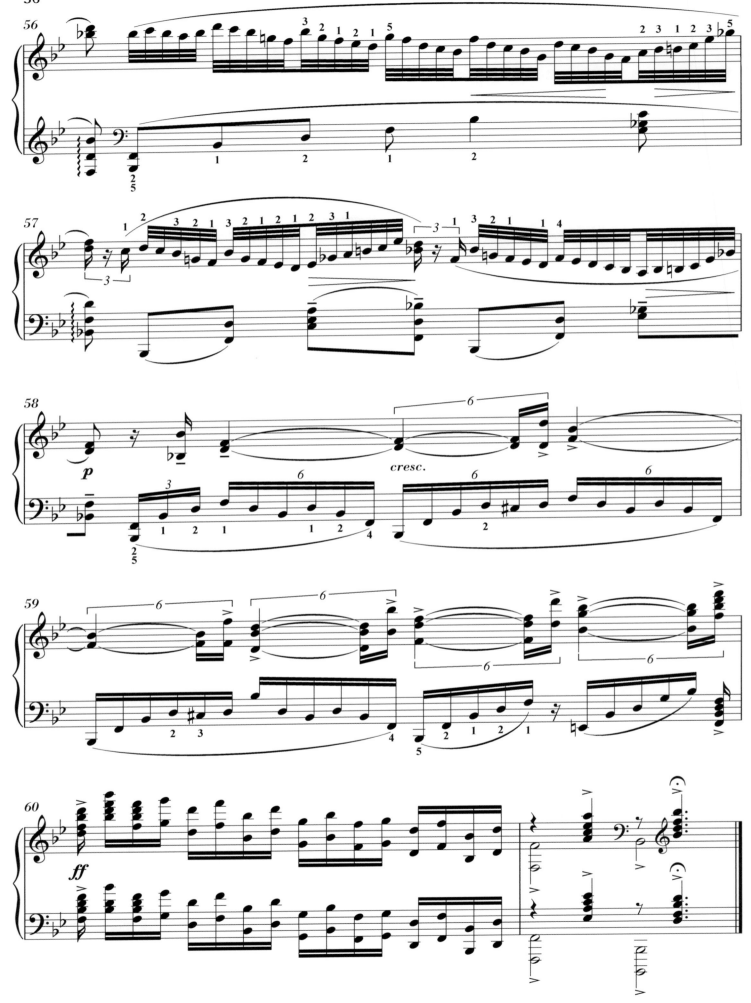

III

Sergei Rachmaninoff
Op. 23, No. 3

Copyright © 2012 by G. Schirmer, Inc. (ASCAP) New York, NY
International Copyright Secured. All Rights Reserved.

Un poco più mosso

IV

Sergei Rachmaninoff
Op. 23, No. 4

Copyright © 2012 by G. Schirmer, Inc. (ASCAP) New York, NY
International Copyright Secured. All Rights Reserved.

*Play the C-sharp with the knuckle, the D with the tip of the thumb.

*See note for measure 16.

*See note for measure 16.

V

Sergei Rachmaninoff
Op. 23, No. 5

Copyright © 2012 by G. Schirmer, Inc. (ASCAP) New York, NY
International Copyright Secured. All Rights Reserved.

VI

Sergei Rachmaninoff
Op. 23, No. 6

Copyright © 2012 by G. Schirmer, Inc. (ASCAP) New York, NY
International Copyright Secured. All Rights Reserved.

VII

Sergei Rachmaninoff
Op. 23, No. 7

Copyright © 2012 by G. Schirmer, Inc. (ASCAP) New York, NY
International Copyright Secured. All Rights Reserved.

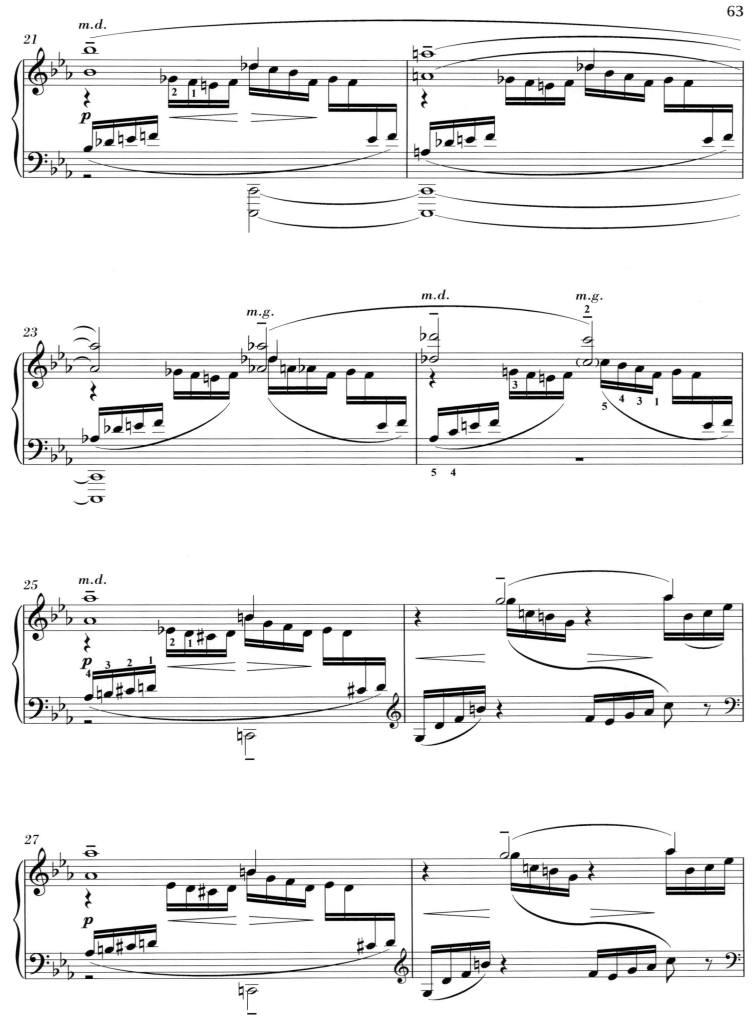

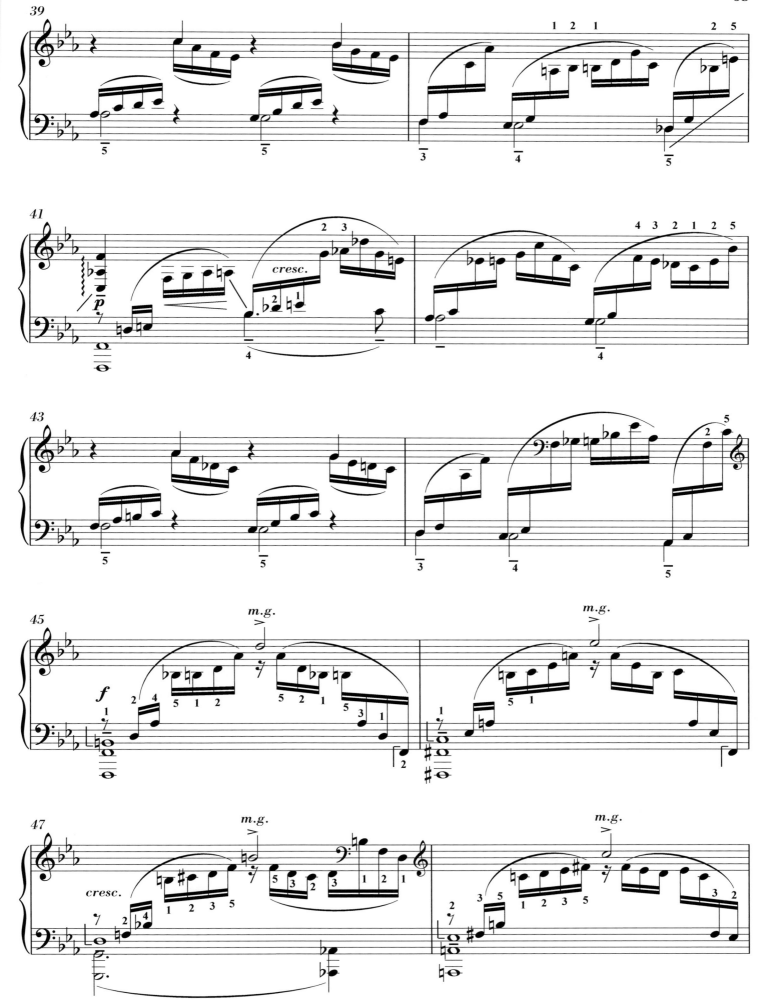

il basso ben marcato

VIII

Sergei Rachmaninoff
Op. 23, No. 8

Allegro vivace (♩ = 108)

Copyright © 2012 by G. Schirmer, Inc. (ASCAP) New York, NY
International Copyright Secured. All Rights Reserved.

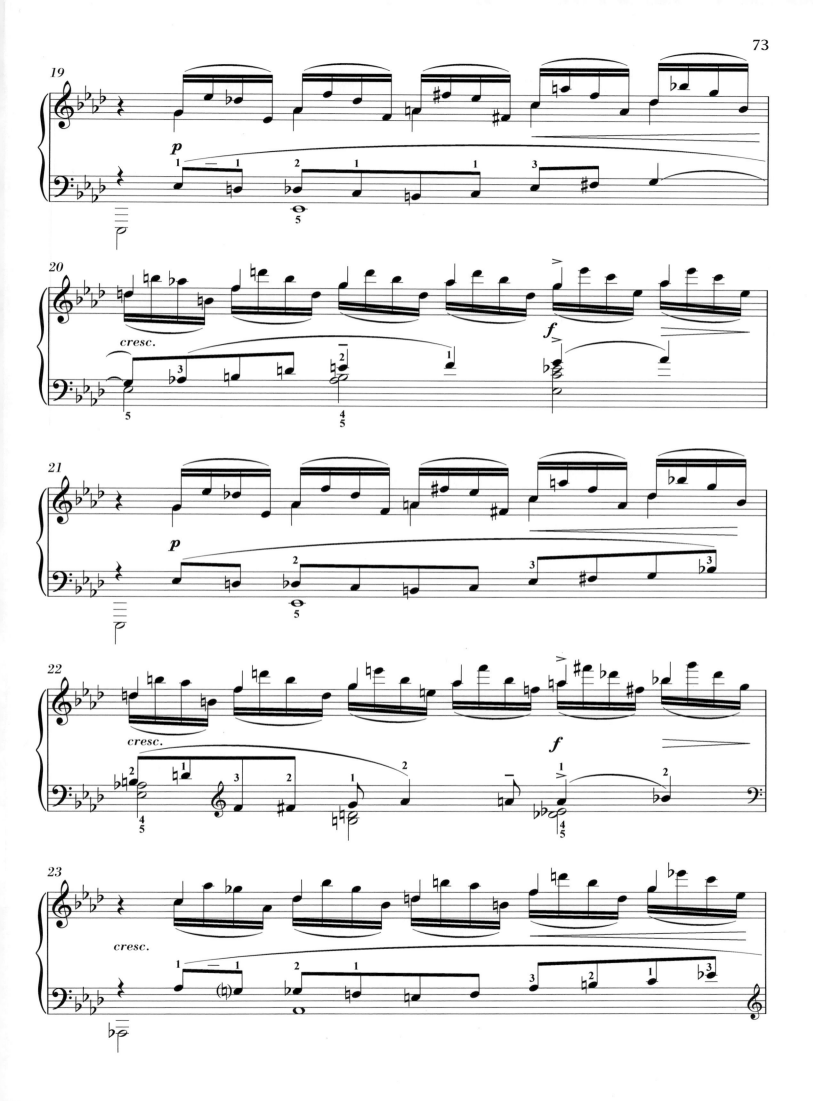

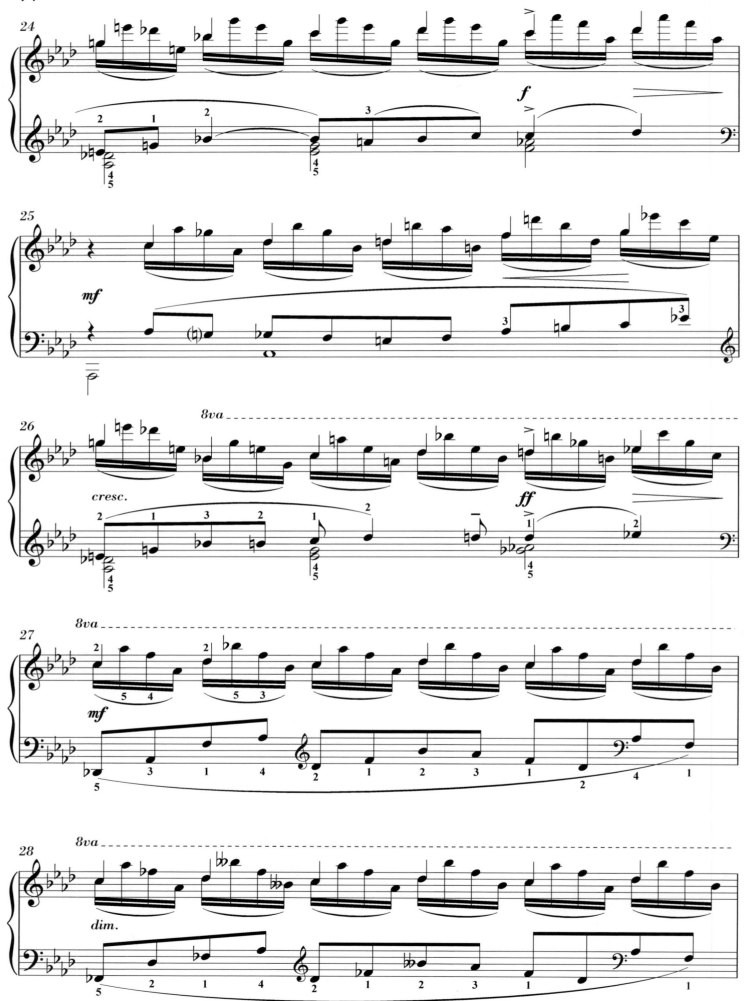

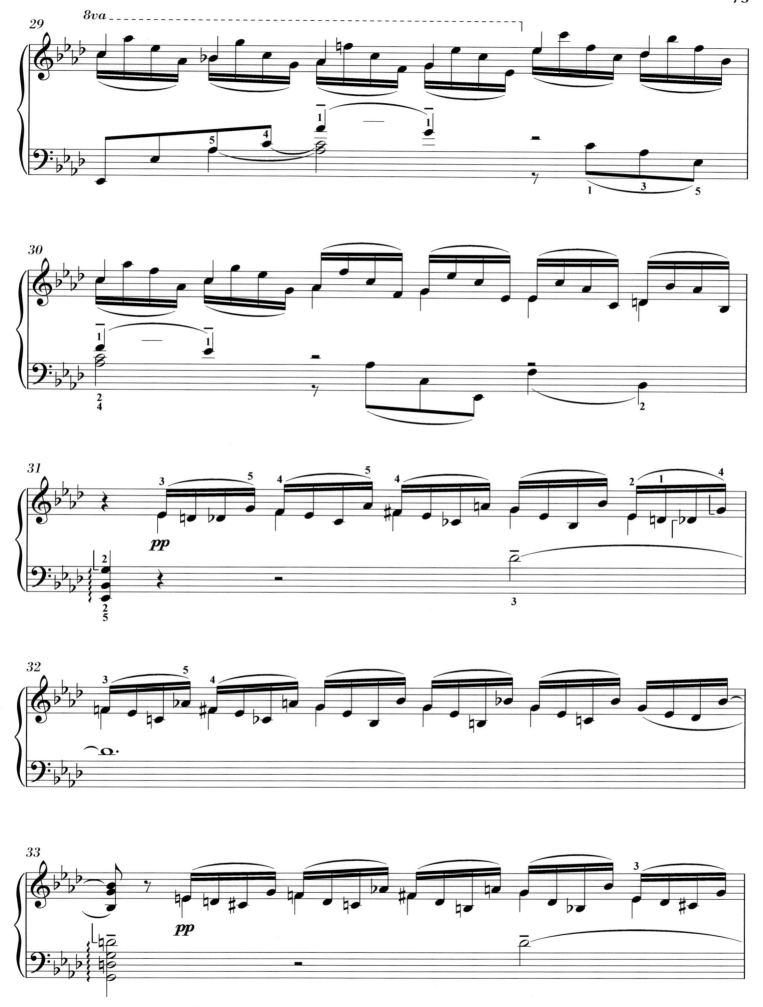

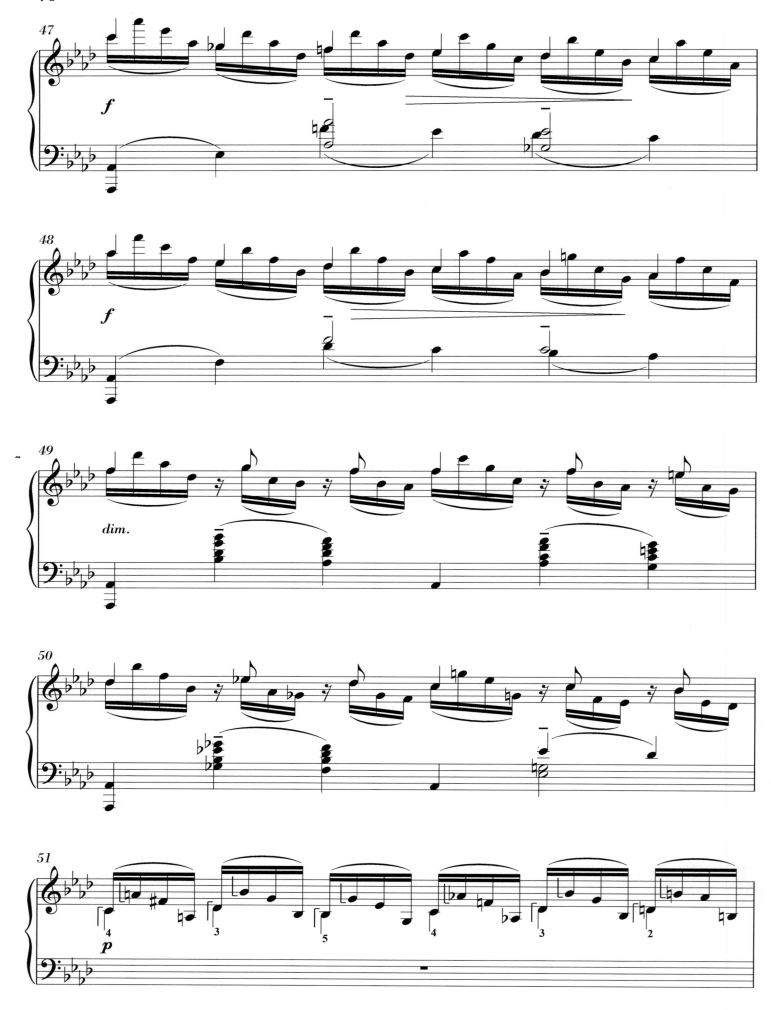

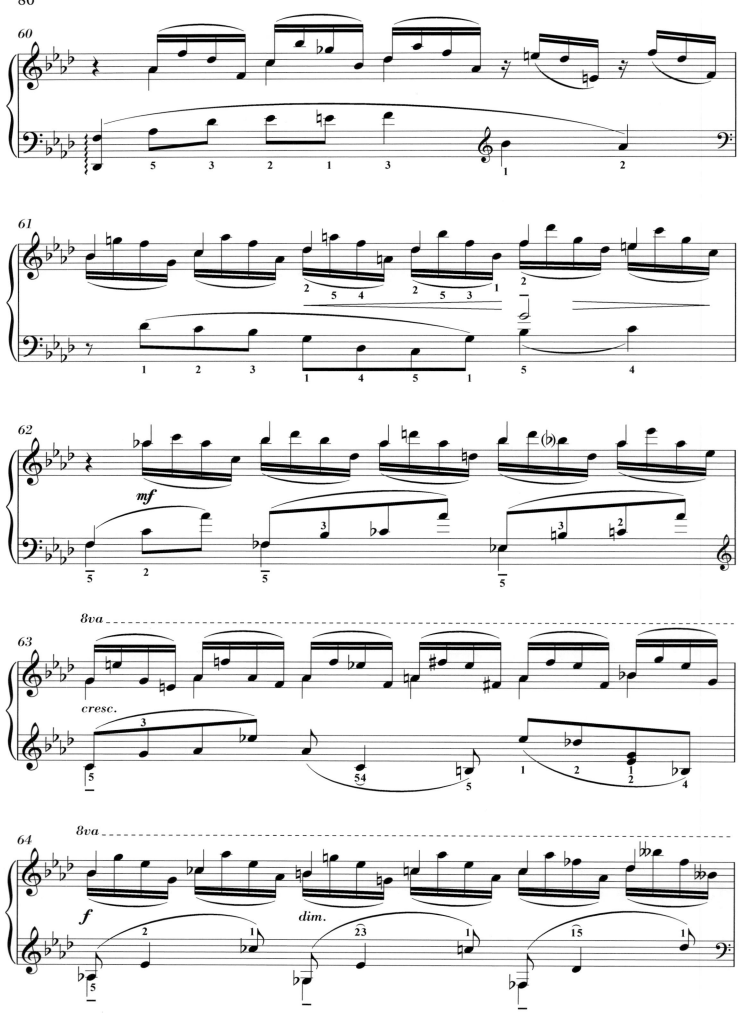

IX

Sergei Rachmaninoff
Op. 23, No. 9

Copyright © 2012 by G. Schirmer, Inc. (ASCAP) New York, NY
International Copyright Secured. All Rights Reserved.

X

Sergei Rachmaninoff
Op. 23, No. 10

Copyright © 2012 by G. Schirmer, Inc. (ASCAP) New York, NY
International Copyright Secured. All Rights Reserved.

*Some editions have **p**.

Preludes, Op. 32
I

Sergei Rachmaninoff
Op. 32, No. 1

Allegro vivace [♩ = 80]

Copyright © 2013 by G. Schirmer Inc. (ASCAP) New York, NY
International Copyright Secured. All Rights Reserved.

II

Sergei Rachmaninoff
Op. 32, No. 2

Copyright © 2013 by G. Schirmer Inc. (ASCAP) New York, NY
International Copyright Secured.   All Rights Reserved.

III

Sergei Rachmaninoff
Op. 32, No. 3

Copyright © 2013 by G. Schirmer Inc. (ASCAP) New York, NY
International Copyright Secured.   All Rights Reserved.

IV

Sergei Rachmaninoff
Op. 32, No. 4

Copyright © 2013 by G. Schirmer Inc. (ASCAP) New York, NY
International Copyright Secured. All Rights Reserved.

Tempo I

V

Sergei Rachmaninoff
Op. 32, No. 5

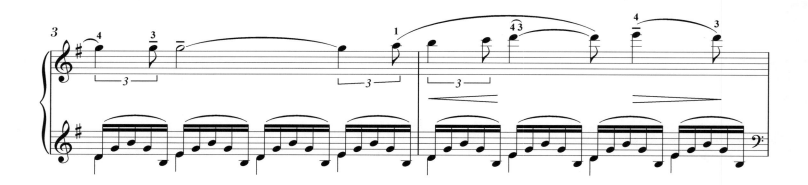

Copyright © 2013 by G. Schirmer Inc. (ASCAP) New York, NY
International Copyright Secured.   All Rights Reserved.

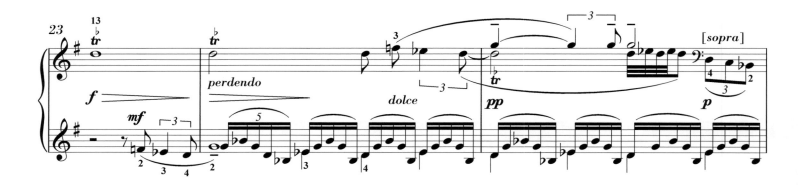

VI

Sergei Rachmaninoff
Op. 32, No. 6

Allegro appassionato [♩ = 100]

Copyright © 2013 by G. Schirmer Inc. (ASCAP) New York, NY
International Copyright Secured.   All Rights Reserved.

* See performance notes for this prelude (pg. 7).

VII

Sergei Rachmaninoff
Op. 32, No. 7

Copyright © 2013 by G. Schirmer Inc. (ASCAP) New York, NY
International Copyright Secured. All Rights Reserved.

VIII

Sergei Rachmaninoff
Op. 32, No. 8

Copyright © 2013 by G. Schirmer Inc. (ASCAP) New York, NY
International Copyright Secured.   All Rights Reserved.

* See performance notes for this prelude (pg. 8).

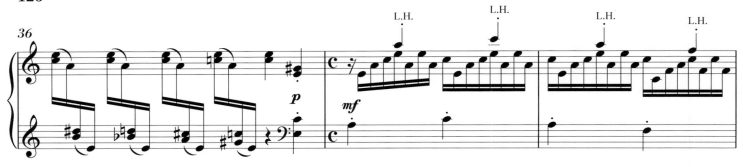

IX

Sergei Rachmaninoff
Op. 32, No. 9

Allegro moderato [♩. = 60]

Copyright © 2013 by G. Schirmer Inc. (ASCAP) New York, NY
International Copyright Secured.   All Rights Reserved.

* Play the lower two notes with the thumb; use the knuckle for the black key, and the nail for the white key. Also in similar places.

X

Sergei Rachmaninoff
Op. 32, No. 10

Lento [♩ = 50]

Copyright © 2013 by G. Schirmer Inc. (ASCAP) New York, NY
International Copyright Secured.   All Rights Reserved.

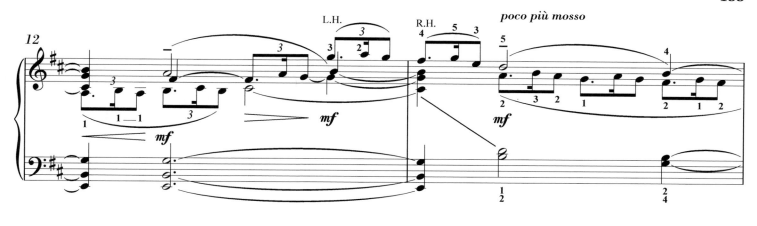

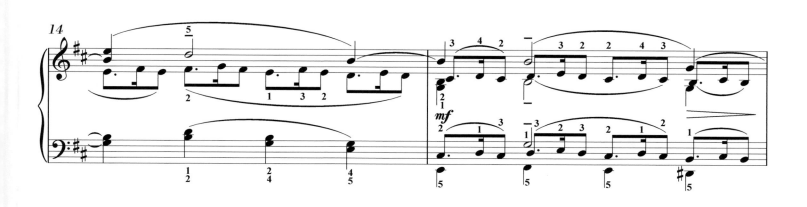

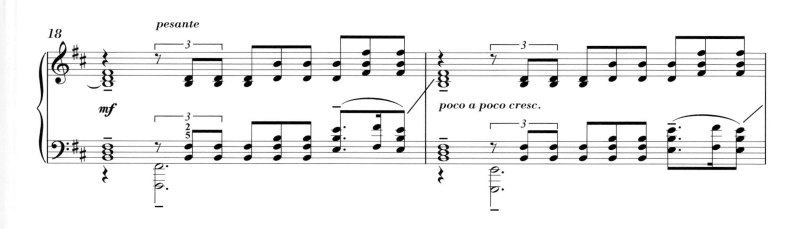

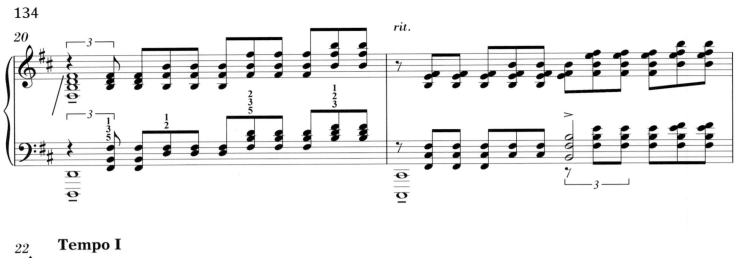

Tempo I

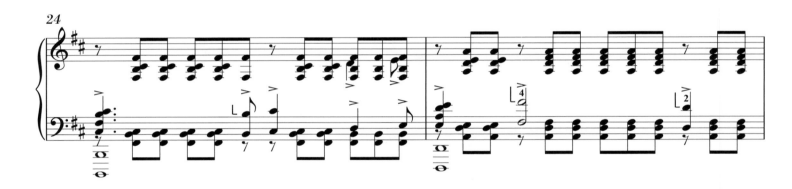

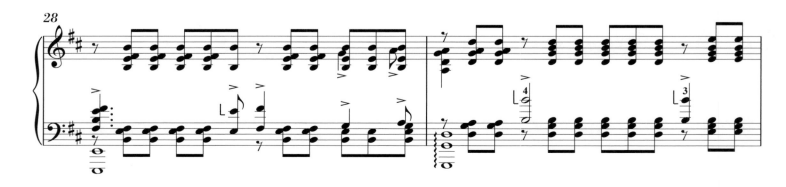

A tempo, come prima

XI

Sergei Rachmaninoff
Op. 32, No. 11

Copyright © 2013 by G. Schirmer Inc. (ASCAP) New York, NY
International Copyright Secured.   All Rights Reserved.

XII

Sergei Rachmaninoff
Op. 32, No. 12

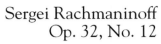

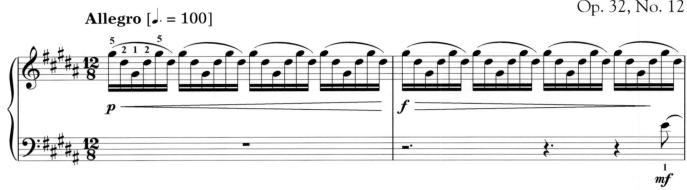

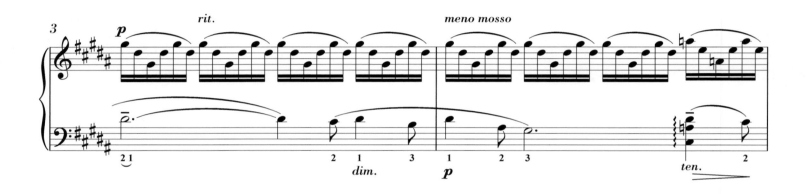

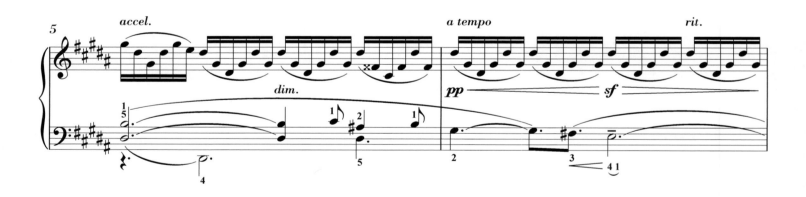

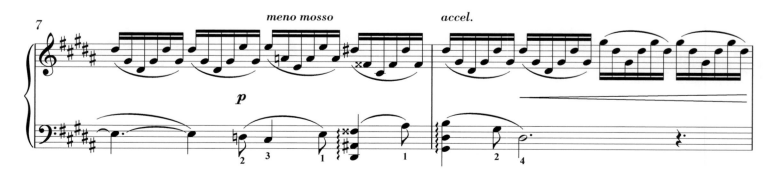

Copyright © 2013 by G. Schirmer Inc. (ASCAP) New York, NY
International Copyright Secured.   All Rights Reserved.

* See performance notes for this prelude (pg. 9).

XIII

Sergei Rachmaninoff
Op. 32, No. 13

Copyright © 2013 by G. Schirmer Inc. (ASCAP) New York, NY
International Copyright Secured.   All Rights Reserved.

* Some editions print G-flat.

* The B-flat may be omitted.

* Some editions print *f*.

ABOUT THE EDITOR

ALEXANDRE DOSSIN

Considered by Martha Argerich an "extraordinary musician" and by international critics a "phenomenon" and "a master of contrasts," Alexandre Dossin keeps active performing, recording, and teaching careers.

Born in Brazil, where he lived until he was nineteen, Dossin spent nine years studying in Moscow, Russia, before establishing residency in the United States. This background allows him to be fluent in several languages and equally comfortable in a wide range of piano repertoire.

Currently on the faculty of the University of Oregon School of Music, Dossin is a graduate from the University of Texas-Austin and the Moscow Tchaikovsky Conservatory in Russia. He studied with and was an assistant of Sergei Dorensky at the Tchaikovsky Conservatory, and William Race and Gregory Allen at UT-Austin.

A prizewinner in several international piano competitions, Dossin received the First Prize and the Special Prize at the 2003 Martha Argerich International Piano Competition in Buenos Aires, Argentina. Other awards include the Silver Medal and Second Honorable Mention in the Maria Callas Grand Prix and Third Prize and Special Prize in the Mozart International Piano Competition.

He performed numerous live recitals for public radio in Texas, Wisconsin, and Illinois, including returning engagements at the Dame Myra Hess Memorial Concert Series. Dossin has performed in over twenty countries, including international festivals in Japan, Canada, the United States, Brazil, and Argentina, on some occasions sharing the stage with Martha Argerich. He was a soloist with the Brazilian Symphony, Buenos Aires Philharmonic, Mozarteum Symphony, and São Paulo Symphony, having collaborated with renowned conductors such as Charles Dutoit, Michael Gielen, Isaac Karabtchevsky, Keith Clark, and Eleazar de Carvalho.

Dossin has CDs released by Musicians Showcase Recording (2002), Blue Griffin (*A Touch of Brazil*, 2005), and Naxos (*Verdi-Liszt Paraphrases*, 2007; *Kabalevsky Complete Sonatas and Sonatinas*, 2009; *Kabalevsky Complete Preludes*, 2009; *Russian Transcriptions*, 2012), praised in reviews by *Diapason*, *The Financial Times*, *Fanfare Magazine*, *American Record Guide*, *Clavier* and other international publications.

In the United States, Alexandre Dossin was featured as the main interview and on the cover of *Clavier* magazine and interviewed by *International Piano Magazine* (South Korea). He is an editor and recording artist for several Schirmer Performance Editions.

Dossin is a member of the Board of Directors for the American Liszt Society and the President of the Oregon Chapter of the American Liszt Society. He lives in the beautiful south hills of Eugene with his wife Maria, and children Sophia and Victor.

www.dossin.net